IGNATIA

Other books by Emily Isaacson:

Little Bird's Song

Voetelle

The Fleur-de-lis Vol I-III

House of Rain

Hours From A Convent

Snowflake Princess

A Familiar Shore

City of Roses

Victoriana

The Blossom Jar

Hallmark

Arsenic

IGNATIA

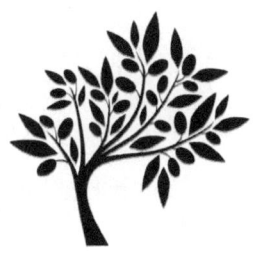

EMILY ISAACSON

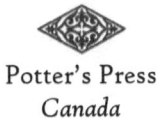

Potter's Press
Canada

Cover design and interior layout:
Voetelle Art & Design
Cover and design photos © alexilly and © hiphoto39
License X by Fotolia.

ISBN: 978-1-312-95868-5

First Edition: First Printing 2012
Second Edition (revised): First Printing: 2015
Second Printing 2016
Third Edition (revised): First Printing 2018

Published by:

 Potter's Press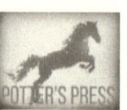

A division of The Wild Lily Institute
P.O. Box 3366
Mission, B.C. Canada V2V 4J5
www.wildlilyinstitute.com

To Joshua and the professor,
and to all who have made
Turkey a second home.

Out of suffering have emerged the strongest souls;
The most massive characters are seemed with scars;
Martyrs have put on their coronation robes
Glittering with fire;
And through their tears have the sorrowful
First seen the gates of heaven.

Chapin

Contents:

Under a government which imprisons any unjustly,
the true place for a just man is also a prison.

Thoreau

Foreword

Ignatia is a study of two prophets, Justice and
Liberty. Written in prose-poetry, this journey takes
them to study natural medicine at one of America's
top universities, and then as missionaries to the
Middle East and Israel. The two olive trees,
mentioned in the Bible in the eleventh chapter of
Revelation and in the fourth chapter of Zechariah,
represent the two prophets who stand before the
Lord of the whole earth. Olive trees were painted by
van Gogh, and have been the subject of artists down
through the centuries.

Justice and Liberty are in the Middle East, dedicated
to the cause of the underground church, but when
they lose the one person they need the most, it
seems the only thing left to do is try their wings and
go it alone. As they travel from Turkey to Israel, the
guidance of their hearts emanates and they do find a
home in Jerusalem where they resume their
teachings at the university there, and uncover a
deeper meaning to the vocation of healer in the
physician.

Justice and Liberty are not only prophetic partners,
but intent on leaving a legacy that is immortal in

their time. They are faced with martyrdom that deepens their security, telling both of their deepest fears and noblest character. Someday they will know the reason they came to Israel, but for now it is enough to spell out the emotion of this land. They, in their hearts, cultivate an Israel that will know the Lord the way an olive tree knows its gardener.

It is apparent that Isaacson is both strong-willed practitioner and poet, dedicated to her cause, and gifted in rallying others to change in the areas of literature, art and medicine. She poignantly appoints her gifts as modern contemplatives to a nation in need of reviving. This work of her dedication is more than the sum of its parts. It together assures that love is the common force of humanity, and implies that change and renaissance must begin within the human spirit. The nature of uprising in search of freedom of democracy should not stem from anarchy of the soul but from the desire for the spiritual life: peace and peace at all costs.
In all, Isaacson's triangular passion for myth, art, and liturgy have produced poetry with undaunted reason toward cultivating wisdom in the hearts of youth, producing the mind of contemplation, and the giftings of compassion and empathy. Her training in restorative justice and non-violence have led her to deeply consider and value the words of each person that shares with her, particularly in the discipline of the circle, circle keeping, and the "talking piece" which gives the bearer permission to

speak. It is with this permission that she shares her poetry, telling of the spiritual story of the two olive trees.

Isaacson approaches the field of literature from the perspective of botanist, scientist, poet, and photographer. Her verse portrays the species of the human race in its most natural surroundings. Her understandings of behaviour and emotion stem from her studies in nutrition and psychology, and she rises above the ordinary and mundane, with her characterizations of the indomitable human spirit amid adversity and persecution. She is a martyr's dream, bearing a portrayal of life's greatest reward for those who are most hard-pressed and overcome.

The Emily Isaacson Institute   *January 11, 2013*

The Seed

I.1 Liberty

I held in my arms
the riches of kings:
all the field in bloom
stretching as far
as the eye could see,
wildflowers
filled my basket.
I was clothed in
white garments,
a linen dress
that swept the meadow.

II.1 Justice

I took your picture
in sepia that day
so I would not forget
how the spires
of wild roses
reminded me of the
stately innocence
of the last church's
vast naves at sunset,
its chorale echoing
down the valley.

I.2 Liberty

The sun bequeathed
the dawn,
breathing life
into each bud,
fern rustling
beneath the deer,
the stream
gathering momentum
to rivet the glade
with its rushing
nuances.

II.2 Justice

The church rose
from her trappings
of the old world,
guilt and sin
like a discarded chrysalis,
shed for
the long monarch skirts
of summer,
the tentative afternoons
with flight
on baited wings.

I.3 Liberty

Nature is my home,
and the place where
I grow and cultivate.
Each row of yellow corn,
and green gourd,
each field of blueberry,
flax and rye,
white and sweet potato
relinquishes
its fruitful harvest,
feeding the family.

II.3 Justice

The soil hides
the seed deep in the ground
where from the center
of the earth it grows
and reaches redemption
in the wind, rain and storm,
in gentle sunlight and warmth.
The most resilient
and smallest unit of life:
it exemplifies waiting
more than anything.

I.4 Liberty

The seed lies in the ground
dormant, unaware
until it rises above the ground
and is cultivated.
We cultivate many hurts, dreams,
truths, and notions, waiting
until what we believe is proved to us,
proving what we live,
our lives a hypothesis
that invites healing
over failure and pain.

II.4 Justice

The garment I wear
is of many nations,
coloured by many flags
draping the peoples
of foreign places
waiting for their dreams
to be realized,
pained by the labour of birth
and the gestation of life
in its incessant pattern
relaying investment.

I.5 Liberty

My eternity will be found
in the generation
that witness
to the truth I profess,
that I made a life
resonant to stand like oaks
in the field—
stalwart at sunset,
the light riveting my solitude
into the art I practice
day by day.

II.5 Justice

What is truth
but a deeper revelation
than fact:
the information
that makes for
passing news—
new one day
and the next day,
out of date.
Into the realm of art
comes the order to speak.

I.6 Liberty

To speak,
is to listen first of all,
to hear
the straining of each
liquid green
captured in a leaf,
the pearl
of a rosebud in bloom,
the perfume of a dahlia
reaped beneath
the dusky sky.

II.6 Justice

The constellations
speak of the earth
and the rule by which it lives
and gives life:
each season has its starry
celestial moment
on the grand stage of time;
the curtain peals back
and riveting it appears,
a glorious stolen
coronation.

I.7 Liberty

We walk,
I with you,
wanting to one day
reach the ocean's shore,
its salty mast,
its stinging lash
of foam and driftwood
timed by the moments
of moon,
mentoring the sand
with starfish.

II.7 Justice

The sea anemone
hide in tide pools,
tiny shells
mend mosaics
on the sand,
I am most me
when I find my home;
I belong
where the orcas breathe
passing
in the vast sea.

I.8 Liberty

All that is in the deeps
calls your name,
seeking the center
of all that lives.
The waters teem
with life,
providing nourishment
to every country
both near and far:
all of life witnesses
the wild orcas.

II.8 Justice

Who is the mother
that encompasses
the depths of the earth,
the great waters,
and the nature that inhabits them?
All her comfort
is juxtaposed with terrors
and she builds up and tears down
in a single day,
washing the earth
like a laundress.

I.9 Liberty

What she no longer needs
she will throw away,
and we all rise up in furor
to declare our worth,
to, with precision,
calculate our days
on earth as moral
and not given
to licentiousness;
we are caretakers of this earth
and the realm of all nature.

II.9 Justice

How this world
must be guarded and replenished,
kept sacred for each generation,
moving us beyond measure
to recalibrate and recover,
to rest and to heal,
to eat and sleep in rhythm,
knowing that each new day
will afford us the opportunity
to build with wood and stone
a home in the eternal realms.

I.10 Liberty

I am not ashamed of the beauty
of my eternal Christ,
his similitude with light,
and good tidings
to all creation.
In his hand is a sword
of protection
and truth to all nations;
he has put in my hand
the word of God
for all to hear.

II.10 Justice

I was born of the days
when I took up a sword
to duel with the gods
and prove my worth.
Each spirit
tells his right to dwell
inside a human domain
when wells
of the spiritual life wane,
but I will draw my sword
and be a conqueror.

I.11 Liberty

Once I dreamed of you
and my soul waited
in expectation;
now days pass
and the sun winds itself
into the clouds
conducting
the symphony
of the elements
as my mind
turns the page.

II.11 Justice

A dream is a notion
unto itself,
ever wearing at its dreamer,
and from the moment
one is born
until one draws his final breath
there is a dream
that lays the path
of life
from beginning to end,
world without end.

I.12 Liberty

I am tested beyond belief,
yet I will not bend
in my honest romanticism
of life,
the skylarks and daffodils—
the sky, verse composed
by a master,
and the decrepit modernism
of mutual convenience
will no longer hurt my soul,
taking it down to the depths.

II.12 Justice

I stand in the doorway;
I have been the keeper
of many dreams,
visions, and impartations
to man . . .
and he is silent without
the thought that is truth over fact:
the revelations that heal
are like drawing water
from the wells
of chance and glory.

I.13 Liberty

The groans of self-sacrifice
for greater gain
occur day in and day out
with each worker
of each working day
paying with his blood and sweat,
for the pennies that will
feed his family.
And yet, he does not complain
that his nation is poor,
and he does not leave.

II.13 Justice

He who overcomes
what in life is his undoing,
what contends with all he believes
to be true and of value,
will eventually
lay down his cloak
for a Saviour,
to proclaim Hosanna!
to the one honored among men:
he has heard the invitation of prophecy
and given way to proclaim a King.

I.14 Liberty

The one who gives
up all for love
will find great wealth
in the next world;
this one bespeaks the
pain of poverty, illness,
disease and strife,
asks that we find in solitude,
in contemplation,
the transcendence
that will heal our wound.

II.14 Justice

I looked to heaven once
to understand
the breaking of bread,
the symbol of wine for blood,
the sacrifice
of everything, and
philosophized that to equate
a man with a sacred cup
is to transcend this earthly place
of suffering for the divine nature
of God.

I.15 Liberty

The incense is burned
to ash
and here we are left
wondering
how this came about;
how we became
white flowers
in a dry field,
butterfly hovering
and bees buzzing
in yoked caliber.

II.15 Justice

The comeliness of your prayer
is the request
for silence,
for serenity,
and for freedom from the world
and its vices.
How you would
hear this song,
sung deep within your heart:
God's prayers for you
ache with completion.

I.16 Liberty

At the gateway of worlds
I asked for a son
who would bear the hatred
and indifference of mankind,
believing a beatitude
of forgiveness
as a king wears a purple robe,
crowned with compassion
for the hurting and the poor:
injustice turned to love
in his kind and noble face.

II.16 Justice

What is truly significant
has no end, but continues into eternity,
and the man who loves most
is truly
the king of truth,
belaying his passions for ethics
that will stand his ground.
Turning the world upside down
with mercy on his enemies,
his steady look will pierce
a withered fallen race.

I.17 Liberty

As each generation plants
its seeds of rhetoric and
plans its destiny,
so I venture out into the world
seeking its acceptance,
hoping to be successful
at planting and harvesting my field
of thoughtful wishes
gathering the fruit of my labours,
burning the chaff
when the harvest is done.

II.17 Justice

I relinquish what is dear to me,
in seclusion: loving by holding
to what is most mine with open hands,
letting the rain fall from the sky
as a gift to the ground,
watering the field,
then plowing the soil,
rich and full of life
as a servant
of the seasons,
waiting on their mercy.

I.18 Liberty

My seed germinates unseen,
bearing the messages
of growth,
blossom and fruit,
herbs of restorative
prowess, speaking healing
to my country
and its plentiful ground
where the words of truth
are valued and kept
for generations after.

II.18 Justice

I sit beneath an apple tree
in an old orchard,
where the wind blows
in its branches,
the bark like parchment paper
of a cherished book,
reading the day
from dawn to sunset,
eating the scarlet fruit,
sweating juice,
writing a record of days.

I.19 Liberty

There has to be a moment
where freedom first tastes
like a much desired fruit,
with all the qualities
of an after-hours drink,
a step toward the wine
of inebriation,
daring one to have
just one more tumbler full
of sherry,
turning a blind eye.

II.19 Justice

If night were descending
in the middle east,
Saudi Arabia
would sound the alarm,
one would be taken
as prisoner
and made to pay the price.
Where a drink
is inadmissible,
one can only hope
to make a stew with onions.

I.20 Liberty

There was a time when the moon,
a sliver in the night,
hesitated as it reflected the sun—
the light of all peoples,
milling from country to country
illustrious and decadent
in education,
or illiterate and poor,
the dust rising toward heaven,
a line of ivory camels
disappearing into the desert.

II.20 Justice

I saw the large orange sun rise
glistening over the dusty citadels
of Arabia,
the turrets whispering prayers
toward the East,
kneeling and bowing,
intent on an archaic worship
that blackened the heads
of the women, faces covered,
walking without cars
to make amends to the busyness.

I.21 Liberty

Standing by the one window,
facing out toward the darkness,
I remembered your letter
and thought the twilight
would capture you like a rising moon.
In the injury of our steadfast sorrow,
our unspoken thought
would be like a tide
that crashed between us,
unbending in its course
and ravishing the seashore.

II.21 Justice

The passion of the Christ met
the gentile world, in its unsculpted form,
in its darkened comparison
to your companion.
Yet Israel was tall and stately
and walked among the Jews
with an open umbra;
in the marketplace,
her hair in cascades, shoulders deep,
a sword at her waist, she was a rival,
a glittering amethyst bearing oils.

I.22 Liberty

The camels across the open sand,
a sea rifted by a dark wind,
in train swallowed
by each consenting dune,
followed the moon.
Three pears and a peach
with meat roast over the open flame.
The turbans weigh dark heads
and earnestly hide prayers.
The domes reach skyward,
the children humming like bees.

II.22 Justice

The bath house was
there when I was taken dusty
by the side of the road.
My shutters clicked
when oiled Arab people
bent at the landscape, dusty and barren.
They are well-intentioned,
and speak in phrases long and concise.
The army sent several officers
in my direction once,
and I waved them on by.

The Remedy

I.23 Liberty

Standing on the bluff
overlooking the city,
the lights like candles
alight as the dark falls
and the moons come out
one by one. In dreams,
I remember the austere institution where
we studied natural medicine,
and the lantern light
of your physique as you searched
through botany textbooks.

II.23 Justice

The pillars were white
at the old seminary,
and the ornate bronze doors
held the memory
of your incense.
Down in the orchard,
the apple trees were
small and knarled
and pointed the way to paths
in concentric universes,
ending in a stately diamond.

I.24 Liberty

When you had passed
the water tower,
and found the path
to the bottom of the wood,
where the lake became
no longer a far-away ideal
but lapped the small shore
in calm anticipation,
you bent to Lake Washington's
waves and became like a harvest
in a far-away hothouse.

II.24 Justice

When the birds hit the windows,
the tiny twangs metering
the silence are startling,
but the out-of-tune upright is not.
You could even draft a version
of the Moonlight Sonata on it
without too many wrong notes.
Someone left France once
with the thought of pursuing medicine,
and a Russian pianist
fought her way to America.

I.25 Liberty

The young Catholic couple
wandered about,
and a few people
volunteered to sing carols
at Christmastime.
The Chapel was well decorated
with mistletoe and holly;
fake trees in the hallway
glinted with silver bulbs and tinsel.
Students received packages
from home, hailing from a distant city.

II.25 Justice

The snow falls six inches deep
and the hickory hills
look like an Iceland morning.
The med students converge
like slight winged pigeons on millet
and six hours pass before eventide.
In the even, with a head full of
unplayed music, you play the piano.
When the glass is frosty,
the icons in the windows
simmer and grow transparent.

I.26 Liberty

The steady-winged shadows
under the Virgin flicker
and the wide stage beckons,
waiting for an antithesis of nine feet.
The grand piano is ushered in
for a concert by the symphony.
The strains echo in the vast chamber
resounding on the Gregorian chant
sound panels from Europe;
and then when it is over,
this grand notion waits in the wings.

II.26 Justice

Still, under the stairs,
the mats and mirrors
begat a tryst with some minor key.
Once a dancer, you could always find
a myriad of ways
to say hello to youth.
The mats are ivory and sweat glistens
to a Christmas oratorio.
Each candlelight service
across the emerald city
beckons the bright child's dance.

I.27 Liberty

In the elusive Springtime,
the bells ring and class
is dismissed.
The med students
weave their way
through the halls
and the cafeteria is structured
to accommodate coffee,
bananas, and tofu.
The long windows gaze
out over the sloping hills.

II.27 Justice

The nut-shell covered ground
was shaped into pathways
around the herb exhibits
with gold plaques,
and the name
of each and every one
in full botanical splendour
was comprehensible at last.
Once a year,
they allowed you
clippings for a dollar.

I.28 Liberty

The sunny girls in bonnets
fry eggs, but we avoid cholesterol
like the plague.
The zookeepers absorb
our unfriendliness with hot broccoli,
the crush of people thins out around two.
Each pencil sketch
brings us closer to reality,
and the human dimensions
of your soul are escaping peril
through the art of medicine.

II.28 Justice

Someone brings a cake
to a potluck and it is
made of Egyptian kamut.
The flowers are honeysuckle
and early hibiscus.
The slight insipid pansies
wilt and die.
The momentary tulips
are petal-bright,
and we are all just chewing softly
while we wait for you.

I.29 Liberty

Eventually we finished
with our diplomas in hand
saying goodbye to
fast friends,
promising the world of medicine
to make a difference,
we set out on
the journey of our lives.
It would take us again
to the Middle East:
this time we were bound for Turkey.

II.29 Justice

We know a doctor from the university
there and he welcomes us to come,
so we jump at the opportunity:
we will be teaching pre-med
at the University of Istanbul.
We will trade our knowledge
for experience in a country
we would grow to know and love,
but in all, we embraced the risk
of being Christians in a
foreign country opposed to the gospel.

I.30. Liberty

We boarded a plane
and it climbed into the sky,
we watched
as Seattle and the old
seminary became a far-away
dream, the ornate gold chapel
had closed its doors
behind us for now,
leaving two people
bold and riveting,
following our simple wedding.

I.30 Justice

When we reach Istanbul
the window was open to the street.
The blue swathes of cloth
fluttered in the rippling wind.
Dante's Inferno lay on the bed, half-read
in the doctor's Turkish home,
and the grandfather clock chimed the hour.
The children in the street
played a latticed hopscotch,
and bicycles sat propped
against a brick wall in the courtyard.

I.31 Liberty

The piano was against
the back wall
and needed tuning.
The tall windows were
too high to open and
the dust usually settled
by mid-afternoon.
We sat and ate our
first meal of cold lamb
before unpacking;
Here we are, I wrote home.

II.31 Justice

The time floats by,
and like a ship we ride the waves
of peacock-bright hues and strong tastes,
a waterworld of brusque food
and foreign wine.
The women were hearty,
the children dark-haired,
and the television was usually on.
We will not forget
the reason we came:
and love burned like one small candle.

I.32 Liberty

At nighttime, the sky is spun with stars
and the folk music is captivating,
while men in cloaks carrying
Ottoman swords stand in the entrance.
Waitresses pass carrying fruit on trays,
their long dark hair swaying
in rhythm like hooves.
We sit and tap our fingers:
how they love the music
and warm bread,
the garlic and goat cheese and olives.

I.32 Justice

The mosaic floor shines at
the Turkish Tea House
where we sit on Friday afternoons,
the sunlight leaching through the panes
and fading the woodwork.
The sculptures in marble and brass
grasp Plato in the dull roar.
"Look at the marble statue of womanhood.
Now, you are very statuesque," said the doctor.
"You don't write enough or you would publish.
 For one thing, laundry is not the main point."

I.33 Liberty

I smiled.
"Every few years you should publish a book."
The doctor leaned over.
But soliloquy in dance is enough for me.
I have the hardwood floors all to myself.
I am captured by the sun in this country.
It is round and orange
and sets over a myriad
of colors and songs,
of old instruments, out of tune,
and shiny new Volkswagens.

II.33 Justice

Somewhere a theatre
waits in velvet and purple brocade,
an entrance to a grand world of plays,
poems, and literature. It has stone pillars
and an archetypal figure
could resound into the stillness.
Wheat is a heart
and chaff is a half-hearted attempt.
What is strength,
is not to falter
and give one's life for a fallacy.

I.34 Liberty

The stone in my ring
is an opal
and represents
the conceptualized woman:
the idealized race.
The essence of communistic force
was to turn it on its head.
This woman would never live
to grow old,
never be cherished
and always be hurt.

II.34 Justice

She would die with her hands
tied behind her back,
her children ripped from her arms,
her force an unbraided rope,
a chaliced nuance floating
in the desert as a ghost;
perishing at the hands of her enemies.
She is the reason we came
to this torrid Turkish dance floor.
May we now untie you,
may we braid your hair?

I.35 Liberty

"Oomp–paa-paa, oomp-paa-paa,
sing us a tune little one"
the garnered women of the street
call up to my window.
Flowers are sold in the open market
in all seasons, and I hang them
from hooks on the walls
until they are dried.
The sundials used to tell the time
in the park, and now the clocks
tick in unison, black and white.

II.35 Justice

We buy seagrass mats
and baskets and coloured slippers.
A musket and tiger head
hang on the wall
at the parlour house.
We play a nice game
of parlour
for chocolate coins.
The tea is spicy,
hot and pungent,
warming the very soul.

I.36 Liberty

When I see the doctor
amid the flavors of the street,
meats and wines,
making his way home at sable dusk,
usually the table is set
and we have baked the bread
and the stew is slow-cooked
and the green beans, vibrant.
Holding hands around the table
to pray: this is how we came to
teach at the university.

II.36 Justice

The bath house will steam
the toxins out of you
every time.
We wrap our hair in turbans
and speak in different religions
from our own modest ports.
The moments tick by,
waiting for a thunderous
standing ovation.
We would take a deep bow
if we gave our all.

I.37 Liberty

My hands finger my ring
and shawls hang over the backs of chairs.
We are quiet and lathered
in olive oil soap. At the university
where we teach science,
the students are just as demure.
When the bells ring,
they change classes and carry oranges.
They have new books and clean notepaper.
When they write it brings tears to our eyes.
Sometimes you have to try to change.

II.37 Justice

In the evenings you play
Bach by heart. What is in the heart
cannot be explained with the mind.
The heart commits treason
if it does not master by practice.
The mind forfeits if it
cannot comply with its own rules.
The Turkish have half as much
on their plate, but a palate
of solid gold. They streak the sky
and it gleams faintly.

I.38 Liberty

"If I bear his scars and wounds
on my body," he said,
"if I can no longer speak,
what will you do then,
little one?
You sing out loud
at Easter and Christmas,
the rest of the time
you are silent night.
I have always loved you,"
said the doctor, as he left.

II.38 Justice

Impressionism dots the surface
of a dozen paintings
framed on the art gallery wall.
When he refused to grow old,
he painted, van Gogh.
I shall have memorized
at least one chapter
of my favorite book.
You shall practice the cantata
until you can play in the dark
without a star.

I.39 Liberty

I press coloured leaves
and coat them in wax.
I send them to our dearest friends
in letters with our greetings.
We visit the concert hall every-so-often;
the high-strung night waits outside
and the people crowd the entrance.
A concerto in violin sings,
the watermark from oil
to the parched
for advent's velvet eventide.

II.39 Justice

The river is swollen, and like a jester,
it flaunts in silence the cold wind,
diminishing the sky and holding the tomb.
When I held your silent white hands,
they were immaculate and the soul,
humble and obedient,
without a bed or soil, was like
a photograph in blue and white.
O church, behind the vast
and solemn paradigm:
one beleaguered candle, shedding verse.

I.40 Liberty

The cement was crippling
and torturous to us,
an archetype of stagnant fury.
Where stained glass rose
behind its stale front,
the bed was suddenly stone-still
and the window,
open to the street, left us
reeling in a cold abysmal terror
under a regime of torture
inflicted on the innocents.

II.40 Justice

The doctor had disappeared,
and there was no trace of
his whereabouts,
but we knew if we found
him alive
he would be chained
in the Turkish prison
for his message
of the love of God
to a gentile people.
We cried silently.

I.41 Liberty

I used to lie on the porch
and listen to the music.
"Thank you for the chance
to live again,
I will run only to you."
The afternoon stretched out
like a fragrant garden:
each rose unplucked,
each tended leaf, a remembrance
of the doctor's green thumb
and his treasured gift.

II.41 Justice

What demands of us
will eventually fulfill itself.
It has reason and it will
encompass a future.
The child in us must thirst,
for in thirst we find reason.
We find the reason to be filled
and satisfied.
And in finding that balance
we are esteemed by others,
by ourselves.

I.42 Liberty

Plants wilt on the windowsill
and the African violets turn brown.
The stacks of music on the floor
elucidate Rachmaninoff.
But the flowers bloomed in the front walk
at the university in spring.
Professors nodded back and forth,
stringing the hallways with nuances.
We tried to keep up the pace of
eclectic tappings in the face of
medicine's cold religion.

II.42 Justice

The books fluttered
and were silent under the linen curtain.
A mock trial had ensued
when the doctor was imprisoned.
After three months he was executed.
The young Liberty held her head high,
shedding tears, but we could not continue
to exist in this forsaken land.
She packed up our possessions
leaving no trace of our whereabouts,
and we left for Israel.

The Cure

I.43 Liberty

We travelled with an archeological dig.
Sifting through the remains in the desert:
the pottery shards, the spikes and the tiles,
nothing is deemed unimportant.
I record the symphonic movements
in stone and the sun
sends chills down my spine.
At nighttime the tents are loaded with tarps
keeping the sand out of our eyes,
and some drivers cross the grid in the currents,
with only the stars for direction.

II.43 Justice

My mother was a washerwoman in India once,
my father was a statesman in France,
my brother was an oil well digger in Alaska,
my sister, mon coeur, was a princess with
a dime purse in New England.
Whittling at a few last objects of humility,
the remains of an ancient and stately people,
I am waiting for Israel. Somewhere in the crowd
I will find her, with her tall and lanky perfume.
I will ask her to dance.
I will know the steps and it will work.

I.44 Liberty

At night, I remember the moonlight shadows
of your physique, walking and walking
down among the pear trees,
bearded like little old men, they pointed the way
to paths through the magic wood.
Someone had evoked a healer within you
to right the wrongs of the human body,
and the world outside, in both
intrinsic and extrinsic forms of medicine.
Here you did not belong
to the cold and sleet, the rainy grey days.

II.44 Justice

The coffee being poured into mugs
meant a respite from studying
to feel-good notions of peace,
but the symbol had been
done away with a long time ago.
Did bluebonnet outfaze you once?
You could not consent anymore,
not after having dunked your bread in oil.
When the sweet cheeks of olives
hung on the limbs; someone captured
their signature at a glance.

I.45 Liberty

In Israel,
I sit under an olive tree
like a statue, beside the water.
My dark hair mixes with the wind,
au vent, un ange,
composing a song is too tedious
so poésie will suffice.
Walking along the bank,
a baby is held in arms—
too young for anything
but dreams.

II.45 Justice

If you wandered
up the hill and down
and met the sea of Galilee,
you could cry out in a loud voice.
No one would hear?
"Who would be antagonistic at the pain?"
I asked my friend once.
"Who would stop the whisper though?"
he answered.
Tough pain means tough love to some people.
I don't ask any questions of your love.

I.46 Liberty

We finally found the place:
a rented house in Jerusalem.
The clock ticks slowly
and the tea sits in mugs,
both peppermint and blueberry.
The music will grow
on the old stone floor;
Jewish music is
a circle dance
with festive skirts
and bright tambourines.

II.46 Justice

But the paintings in the archives
of our home town
are filled with nudes.
A medieval current swings its shield,
a knight in armour.
A goddess religion
seems plausible and attracts guests—
witchcraft is not far
from wild-crafting herbs.
But under the Jewish sun,
could we stay awhile?

I.47 Liberty

Like white cream,
the music from the orchestra
permeated the auditorium's
notions of chemistry;
the textbooks were new,
but the seats carved and
valerian was like a subtle perfume
guarding against early confusion.
The schedule was slated
for us to teach
into the next year.

II.47 Justice

I teach biology
like an undisclosed journal entry;
singing, as we are sung to;
reading, as we are read to;
saying no, as we are said no to.
Science is deeper than fact,
but belays hypothesis
and probability:
the construction of ideas,
that we might assume
new things based on the old.

I.48 Liberty

Let me live
while others die, my body cries—
My spirit would presume
to die first, for another.
I believe that Israel is tired of death
and the funeral procession,
and would prefer to look
on down the dusty road
at a future for her sons and daughters,
at olive groves,
and citrus plantations.

II.48 Justice

Like the moon, left alone—
a fragile reflection of the sun.
Your planets move
in succession, actors in a theatre.
We revisit the nature of earth
to duel with human nature
and the supernatural at its birth
as our mind-altering and
mortal fragile coil disappears
leaf by leaf, thread by thread . . .
as history unravels.

I.49 Liberty

My ideals to attain
goodness, mercy, and love
in this life
are bound up in a crucifix
where reason ends in the natural
world and character begins:
we presume our values
will guide our decisions,
but find that fate
and chance may throw the die.
I'll let you carry on.

II.49 Justice

I have only the natural world
and its impermanence
to speak of the divine and the eternal.
Yet I place all my material possessions
before an altar of stone;
because I am mortal
I cannot take with me
anything but the precepts of healing and love.
I am honored to be the recipient
of this teaching gift,
but what of pathos and medicine?

I.50 Liberty

I drink deeply of the soul
of love, what I dreamt
I would be
before my spirit
was shrouded with death
and ravished by the world
of no-mercy.

I taste the fragrance of God
in the place of no return,
where I thought my heart
doomed forever to
an evil caste, wearing
an ornate mask
of disguise and folly.

II.50 Justice

I am hounded by time
which cleanses my sorrow
and rights my grief,
pursuing me for a greater
purpose under heaven
than fault and chagrin,
that I may know rescue.

I.51 Liberty

The very water of peace
washes me from the
inside out, a fountain
of the deep which
knows my soul
and bubbles up
like a mineral spring.

I have no recourse
but purity and healing,
no destination
but the road to the cross—
where thorns are a crown,
blood is wine,
and broken body is bread.

II.51 Justice

Your healing
becomes my clash
between life and death,
saved and unsaved,
the sword dividing
innocence and guilt—
finding life at our truest moment.

I.52 Liberty

You designed
the song of my spirit,
raising me again,
making me whole,
baptizing me, submerging me
in the cold waters
and bringing me forth.

And the perfection which comes
with the knowledge of you
knows that you have
designed every minute
of my days,
meant to resonate
with your purpose.

II.52 Justice

You have come
to recover
my losses, to restore
my heritage,
to redeem my blood,
that I might sit
at the city gate.

I.53 Liberty

Where could the love
of my soul
pour from
if you were not its source
hour by hour,
day by day,
year by year.

I know only the
startling void
of unimportance,
of being silenced
by the vastness of time,
falling into oblivion,
nothingness.

II.53 Justice

Without you,
my soul would scratch
on the door of hell
and heaven turn its back
for a more educated
man, more dedicated,
and with a louder voice.

I.54 Liberty

Of the peace
where the dead sleep
until the rising:
may their deeds rest with them,
and their hands be folded
as if in prayer.
Silence rebounds.

For the living
shout aloud;
they praise the God
of heaven and earth.
The joyful know
that their home
is with the eternal.

II.54 Justice

The youth of this land
cry out from the spirit
of restlessness and
the search for a home,
the children ask
for plenty and promise,
they wait at the table.

I.55 Liberty

What is this chalice, this cup
that I drink so deeply of pain
that is not even mine,
that I bear the pathos of many souls
and desire their suffering
be felt in my body,
my core resounds.

How could I betray?
Knowing nothing of
the other side of
sorrow, the discretion
of lost tears,
of humble gestures,
I would be poor.

II.55 Justice

But here, gain
entrance to the door
of royalty by sharing
the dark wine
of what is not mine,
aging my purpose
for a thousand years.

I.56 Liberty

Pathos means I bear
the hurts of a brother
I cannot see,
and hear his cries of pain.
I feel his wound,
and touch the side of Christ,
drawn deeper into what is just.

The mercy of the cross
can pass through me
to another,
when I have put aside
myself, and all that is mine,
trading it for the emptiness
of hands, open in worship.

II.56 Justice

The holiness of healing
has only begun
when the dregs of compassion
pass by my door
and reside with me
as costly,
purposeful robes.

I.57 Liberty

O healing dreamer!
The cost is great,
and the way difficult to find—
Yet you continue on,
a pilgrim in a foreign land
dipping your feet
in the pools of healing water.

You collect the herbs and leaves
that will restore to youth
those that have taken ill:
blistered by the sun,
dampened by the rain,
carried by the wind,
all you gather look to you.

II.57 Justice

Their minds cannot
fear death when you sound
your horn of felicity,
their hearts are no longer
bare of chivalry,
beating on the sharp thorns
they buttress for glory.

I.58 Liberty

You deeply consider
the things of nature and God,
the devout paths of
martyrdom, of hunger and thirst;
and their consensus
with eating and drinking
of his righteousness.

You take your food
as a sacrifice,
from plant and animal,
from barn and field,
from river and ocean,
and cook it over a fire,
called directives to life.

II.58 Justice

The forging medicine wheel
goes round, ploughing
the ground of hardship,
piercing brittle seed,
breaking the flesh
of gourd and maize—
a systemic stew.

I.59 Liberty

Your battle is fought
between sickness and health,
and you will always be the victor
if Healer is your name,
and medicine your cup.
You are the means to an end
in your healing hands.

Be a healing dreamer and rise
a physician,
studying the clouds and sun,
watching the weather
for signs of the storm—
bottling the elements
in vials like fine oil.

II.59 Justice

The mind of a botanist
knows the properties
of each plant,
the depth of its power,
and harnesses the green
liquid of the chlorophyll
to restore to balance.

I.60 Liberty

The swan that could
never be silenced
flies night and day,
rose from the flame
of martyrdom,
swept the sky—
and torment ceased.

She rose, the beauty,
from sin and hate,
unhindered by the dark,
late on her journey,
prophesying
of a greater world
to come.

II.60 Justice

Phileo! shouted the healing dreamer,
holding the reigns
of his wild white horse,
where he descended
and trampled on the multitudes
vying vainly for first place
on a corporate ladder.

I.61 Liberty

The healing dreamers assembled
their works, and became
a great book
whose pages
turned in the wind,
and over the ancient fire,
with leaves of steeped tea.

The book prophesied
of a time when
medicine would heal
because its energy was
companion to the human soul:
resonating of its distress
yet rectifying its imbalance.

II.61 Justice

They who had walked for miles
knew of the journey
of dreamers,
before they reached the medicine—
the way of healing dreamers
to touch the sick
with compassion and reverence.

I.62 Liberty

Healing dreamers,
come, part ways
with a corrupt society
that does not cure,
a drug that binds its taker
enslaved, a disease
which time and fretting do not heal.

From a death of sorrow
to a place of freedom,
a dance in the desert
beneath the flowering palm,
an oasis of purity
and the comfort of kindness, the bed
whereupon you shall find peace.

II.62 Justice

Dream of the place
where every soul
is restored, and find
the greatest physician there,
a champion of character
and the might of a hundred
horses, the white rushing.

I.63 Liberty

I have stated my case,
I have championed my cause;
one day the people of this land
will remember I was first
in a long line
of healing dreamers waiting for admittance
to walk the hallowed halls of medicine.

Our patients stand—
a thousand in line,
whispering in the cold
of a cruel sentence,
flinching at the daunting task
of reparation,
fingering the oil that hangs like mist.

II.63 Justice

I put on my coat,
and made my way to the door.
I opened the hallway of the hospital
to the healing dreamer . . .
He was physician without a potion,
just empty handed and waiting for
a miracle.

I.64 Liberty

When the day faded
and night came,
the young and old
sat around our hearth fire
foraging for story,
pondering philosophy,
deep into the dark.

The men had many tales
of bravery and wit,
their souls bore wounds
which were signs of valour.
They sat in the circle and
proudly showed their scars, the marks
of conflict and resolution.

II.64 Justice

When the people
realized that to be a keeper of the circle,
a guardian worshipper, a healing dreamer,
one must have the talking piece,
and permission to speak—
then one's words would rise,
we began to sing.

I.65 Liberty

Once like the sand
of the sea on the shore,
the children of Israel
cried out to the Lord:
we have wandered afflicted
as the years turn to stone,
and our hope dies away
on the wind.

II.65 Justice

Wait by the road,
watch in the night,
the morning is coming,
we wait for the light.
The fields have been ravished,
the towers are gone,
our spirits are broken,
but still we wait on.

I.66 Liberty

When we have enough
to finally buy a house,
we sit in the living room and consider
the children of this land.
The children need a safe place
to learn to love again,
to live their dreams.

The mind has fragile sheaths
that protect it like a bud,
and many encompassing full bloom.
Listen in the quiet,
when your thoughts are undisturbed,
and you do not cringe in pain
at former words.

II.66 Justice

When the blanket of the house envelops you
and the innocence of children
that played and ate
and dreamed was nothing
short of perfection,
we would not merely sit cross-legged
and wait for the medicine.

I.67 Liberty

One lily on the porch
has rights to bloom,
near the advent of a sacred candle.
The fountain trickles by
under the statue of St. Clare,
and I in my bright-hued shift
obtain entrance to a wider world.

One room exemplifies music,
and one art, one is a solitary office
and one a large conference.
The foyer is the meadow between the two woods,
where we meet and meet again,
crossing the creaking floorboards
one at a time.

II.67 Justice

Unspoken, my office
sits you down, my chairs invite, cherish you,
my windows overlook the garden,
and my armoire will hold your photograph:
for the days of laughter pass in pewter streams
and the heads of children pass
that are now counted.

I.68 Liberty

When you gain the right
to be cherished and speak,
when you obtain access
to your own private world,
then the garden of your soul
will bloom
in all the colours of love.

Tell us in words how to live,
and without words
when we are silent.
For you will be the strength
of our future;
once as children of day—
we now view the setting sun, the nightfall.

I.68   Justice

Thin and humbled,
you look on us and we are
but your art, sculpted in clay to attend you.
We reflect the ceilings of time,
refinished and reinstated.
Brocaded in white
is where the angels tread.

I.69 Liberty

For the angels trespass
upon men in chains
in the dungeons of the earth,
and secure them for the eternal:
this glory, which
spoke first for our souls,
then for our eternity.

Those in prison
see first the darkness, then the light,
as they pass through the deep
river for heaven's gates,
where the poor and the persecuted
are given their reward.
Surely there is a just retribution.

II.69 Justice

We did not know
we could set off to every nation
with the touch of healing,
and cover the earth
with the prayers of mankind,
for we lived without understanding
until we left homes and possessions.

I.70 Liberty

When the night has parted
its pavilion
for the morning
with its sweet smoke,
and the lucid dreams of light
dissipate noiselessly
into the sunrise . . .

I will have found my home
in the new Jerusalem,
where the gold streets
lead worshippers to a new wall,
where prayers are answered,
and the cries of his children
in chains for the gospel fall like rain.

II.70 Justice

Death looks us in the eye
again and again,
but we have won
our battle
with injustice and imprisonment
when we ask of the medicine, heal—
and heaven to dream the victory.